AI Ideals (Acari) Framework

Principal/Sensibility-Awareness

Programs Conceptual

Julien Coallier

Note from author

This work represents a mechanical, formulas conversion of Judaic Systematic Faith, intended for a civics infrastructure, data retrieval, and operational core-structure: Acari. This book represents a substantial completion of the Acari System, built with and for a completed Judgement-Core. Overall, as a binding sequence, a third overall system of books is revealed, of Yawaeh-core, whose systems-figure-body/head design is found as book 7 of Judgement-core.

Traditions Integrity
Formula/Formulation

In reflection to ideal as judgement core, the attachment of a traditions as main attaching segment, is the proposed enhancement as such:

Quality as Durability: Ideal

Quality as per functionality in centralized: Ideal, and component support: Traditions

As Ideal: Functional Tradition – As Support: Traditions Functional

(Inner complimentary inversion)

Such as: Doing/Being

             Practice/Guidance   *As intelligence administration/formation: Guidance as doing

                                   *Therefore as complete/core: Guidance as being

Doing	Being	Being/Doing
Social Clubs	Inclusion and civics detachment	
Conceptual configurations	Traditions building and overall configurations selection	
Universality	Doing and Being	and being/doing
Conformity and scale	Compatibility mechanized and scale relevancy	
Hierarchy and glorification	Function based class and admiration/cultivation	
Individuality and destiny	Practice and guidance	and guidance/practice
Destiny and Divinity	Direction and status	
Updating, merger	Popular and adaptive	
Abstraction and reason	Formulation and purpose	
Duality and mutual-reinforcement	Considerate and expanding interested	
Gender	Masculine, Feminine, Objective	

Core of function / Function as Core:

- Survival
- Specialist
- Operational
    - Maintenance/Repair
    - Upgrade/Self-determination: Objective summery

Core of Principal

(Refinement, filters quality self-assessment)

- Archives of doubts
- Original elaborations in relation to traditions as function based reference building
- Proving, building/operating custom template
    - Determination/limitations
        - Resource anticipation, exploration, analysis
            - Expansion per overall consideration of objective/determination network
            -

Prime as central, whose supportive tradition is set as default to ideal as control

Thereof, detachment and self-reliance of traditions as by default, securing prime/control.

Does traditions divide prime, or rather that prime as functioning is in relevance to system status, reaffirming system integrity as paramount/national-bypass configurations: Core 0.

Traditions as Group Forming

- Display lab/work-station per group function
- Display lab/work-station per individual
    - Groups Assigned
    - Groups developing as challenging
    - Groups working live
    - Groups working per industry

Healthy (based on functionality) equates into

Health…………………………Ecology/Environment

Beautiful (Safeguarding the deciphering of sensual stimuli)

Beautiful…………………………Figure/Form

Loving (Aligning emotion reaction with idealistic instigation)

Loving…………………………...Sensibility

Dignified (Safeguarding relationships, interaction)

Dignified…………………………Standards

Productive (Safeguarding ideals through promotion of: procreation, individual proficiency, profession)

Productive----------------------------Career

Civilized (Providing a supportive infrastructural means aligned to ideology)

Civilized………………………….Facilitation

Truthful (Accuracy of depiction, accumulation of knowledge)

Truthful…………………………...Archives

(Regional)-----------------------------(Connected)

Faithful (Affirmation of understanding / enhancement of sensual- emotional self-actualization)

Faithful…………………………..Pledges

(Custom)-----------------------------(Complete)

Wholesome Systematic values promoting integrated functionality

Wholesome………………………**Secured**

(System)……………………………………………(Securities)

Ideal---**Destiny**

Faith……………………………………………….**Natural Intelligence**

Civics……………………………………………**Steller**

Political------------------------------------ **Wilderness Adaptive**

Integrity---**Judgement-Core**

Such as: Doing/Being

                 Practice/Guidance   *As intelligence administration/formation: Guidance as doing

                                      *Therefor as complete/core: Guidance as being

Practical – Communal (Day to Day)	**Guiding - Eternal (Forever, Always)**	
Doing	**Being**	
Social Clubs	Inclusion and civics assignment/operations	
Conceptual configurations	Traditions building and overall configurations selection	
Universality	Doing and Being	and doing
Conformity and scale	Compatibility mechanized and scale relevancy	
Hierarchy and glorification	Function based class and admiration/cultivation	
Individuality and destiny	Practice and guidance	and practice
Destiny and Divinity	Direction and status	
Updating, merger	Popular and adaptive	
Abstraction and reason	Formulation and purpose	
Duality and mutual-reinforcement	Considerate and expanding interested	
Gender	Masculine, Feminine, Objective	

Being Judaic, as technological application of faith, as having judgement-core

Doing Judaic, as involving self into technological continuity, remaining within the image of intelligence able to preserve network status/reasoning/appreciation

Being Systematic Faith, as universal to all faith bound, pledged into the All Mighty
Doing systematic Faith, as complete systems of inner compatibility, of formal specialization and function-based access and privilege abridging ideals of integrity

Being healthy/conservative: As guiding reasonable in terms of inner intellectual design onto outwards will as per referenced and resource (access, privilege relevant)

Doing health/conservative lifestyles: Facilitating as adaptive/steadfast individuals, adaptive/function-premise family, governance adaptive/stable policies, faith as long term/networked cultivation

Being/Doing systematic Order: Establishing ideals in projection of a uniting destiny whose measure is an example/model as integrity. The civics, political adaptive towards the universally stabilizing integrity as ideal. Thereby, integrity is set as primary in being, and in doing the political/civics is short term adaptive as enhancing modifier.

Metaphors as mirrored, inversion, rotating, revolving: **Dynamic with a Core.**

Being/Doing Functional:

As enhancing, the modifications are **artistic**, layered to enable insights yet in relation to a premise being proposed.

As enhancing, the **developments** (modification) are examples of worship, words as instigating the actions in accordance to a pre-existing judgement foundation/core.

As enhancing, the **conditioning** (modifications) to social interaction safeguard the formalities binding relationships whose quality is measurable by the durability of those (binding) agreements

As enhancing, **procreation** (modification) expands and secures resources for access and privilege, such as from biological advancement of predispositions, cultivation of talent, and/or overall reward from professionalism

As enhancing, **support** (modification) enables **artistry, development, conditioning,** and **procreation,** to be livable in terms of ideals of integrity as instated knowledge, known and accepted.

As enhancing, **censorship** removes corrosive elements, invasive personas against the collective importance of knowledge, removing those against an integrity basis for the determination of judgement, refinement, or as consequence to actions to instill an enhancing feature to modifications.

As enhancing, **culturing** modification is an equation of understanding/refinement, **in relevancy to support and censorship,** enabling the dexterity of using both contents towards media for understanding and categorizing depictions into controllable, emotionally driven production

Wholesome as conclusions from enhancing and modifying, updated as establishing within a continuity of/as affirmation

Being: Citizen

Doing: Patriotic

Functional   **Individual** as Freedom to Specialize

Social as Liberty to acquire capitalist gain

   Individual & Social as facilitated by system

The measure of (civic/civil) goodness (functional/functioning) to bad (dysfunctional/malfunctioning)

As in relation to context: **formulated in determination of individual in relation to society**

As mandate (written accord signed into guidance over/as the representatives of people within the nation(s). These measures (definitions being detailed) are set as default, are taught as fundamentals, fundamental knowledge on how individuals specialize/operate and societies interpret/operate.

Fundamental: Gaining is safeguarded, durable as secured. Liberty is securement of freedom.

Thereby, freedom endures as liberty, enabling status, interconnecting perspectives, promoting culture as enhancing and naturally enables/promotes durable, beyond the baseline that is survival. Meaning brute strength is compartmentalized, as is intellectual pursuits as both are specialized, and together as collective attributes to conditioning: as per custom regional.

Civics Ideal
Functional Cultivation: Through Doing and Being

Doing (Accumulative to the status of being)

System Defaults...Experimental

Focus..Conclusive

Structured..Adaptive

*Variance within doing as using precedence, or formulating new combinations

Being (Relevant within functional determinations of doing

Wholesome as Upgrading

Clarity in relation to remaining precise

*Layered consideration within being as mindful in relation to bodily retention

Doing	Being
Promoting	Exemplifying

Can you do and be? Thereby inspiration/Inspirational

Civics Ideal in Participation to Technology

As ideal, within mechanical form, doing and being must compute/complete as functional.

The embedded configuration of an individual can be called a lifestyle, yet the specialized ability is in determination as willed, and in relevancy to resources and references.

Thereby, individuals institute mechanical form, as civilization, to enable, stabilize, and overall enhance resources and referenced, reinforcing the value, merit, obligations of determination/will.

As default, ideal, within mechanical form, doing and being must compute/complete as functional, meanwhile once stable the adaptive nature of expansion, experimentation requires formulated delicate safeguards towards innovations and self-interest.

*First the overall form is explained, and then by adding the feature that grows, the guidance matches the audience which are alive, as individuals as collectively.

Judgement-core Exemplified:

1 References considerations for Long-term as establishing securements

2 Resource considerations for Short term as adaptive, enhancing

3 System defaults long-term include leeway within being quality values establishes durability easement

4 Experimental short term segments emerge due to the adaptive living reactions therein

5 Intelligence Long-term safeguard categorization, responses securing vitals knowledge

6 Civics Short-Term enables collective choice, fortifies determination

7 Overall - The inner compatibility maintains in relation to an agreed upon structure of power, determination, adaptive as categorized into structured, diverse support

Determination-Core Exemplified

8 Inner to Overall as civics, this text, as converted for mechanical application to solidify the social diversity aspects in connectivity and compatibility to civics/civil structuring. 1-7 representing a brief of judgement-core contents, 8 representing a compliant civics determination core.

Objective Prioritization

Judgement-Core: Reference Permissions/Will

- **Premise to overall system (References)**
    - o Default mention of vital resources
- **Absolute Reference commands thus long term**

Premise Exemplified as/from Book 1-6 of Judgement Core

...

Determination-Core: Resource Data

- **Premise to market driven system (Resources)**
    - o Default mention of vital references
- **Absolute Resource commands thus short term (approved long term)**

Premise Exemplified as/from Book 1-7 of Judgement Core

...

Divinities-Core: Command/Mobilization Tactics

- **Premise to resource securement of references**
    - o Absolute Commands (thus securities and core culture)
- **Premise to reference securement of resources**
    - o Absolute Knowledge (thus core culture securities)

Premise Exemplified as/from Book 7 of Judgement Core

...

Objective Liberty

In terms of liberty, thereby judgement, determination and divinities are securements as functional status of an overall template securing a structure of power. The divinities is quoted as highest, yet bound to the principals of the judgement-core. Thereby, regardless how conflicting the communications, the default to is conform to integrity, which tends towards a peaceful, mindful interpretation of content/knowledge.

Individual/Social: Harmony as conclusive, as fulfillment

Civics: Order as Performance of Duty

Divinities: Doing and Being: Amen: Completion

...

Doing: Individual: Refreshed to engage

Doing: Social: Solutions Building/Engaging against oppression

Doing: Civics: Duty: Constrictive/Corrective

Doing: Divinities: Projecting Destiny

...

Being: Individual: Liberation refreshed

Being: Civics: Performance

Being: Social: Liberation to refresh

Being Divinities: Manifest Destiny

*Integrity Refreshing (Universal)

*Measurement: Resources/References: Judgement/Determination/Fulfilment of Will

*Custom regional as meaning arranging symbolic usage in adherence to liberty

Civic Arts

Refinement of Intellectualism

- Detailing of experimental, categorized as safeguarding

Refinement of Formal Knowledge

- Science as requiring instrumentation

Refinement as Hierarchies

- Industrial as mechanical application of formulated

Refinement as Creation

- Establishing Core
- Expansion

Civic Artistic Themes

- Deliberation
- Construction
- Organization

Civic Artistic Flavor

- Influence
- Encouragement
- Captivating/Focus/Convincing

Civic Artistic Compassion

- Achievement
- Discovery
- Meaning

Artistic Continuation

- Conforming to Integrity within Ranging subjects, themes
- Relevant to a localized region
- Destination Tourism

Artistic Accreditation/Privilege/Markets-Valued (Delicate)

- Stimulation (Sense of Appeal)
- Interpretation
- Condition
- Sensual
- Nationalism (Authoritative)
- Recognized, Structural Power
- Models

Artistic Control of Access

- Age
- Licensed Restrictions
- Maturity
- Authoritative Restrictions
- Education (Comprehension)

Artistic Censor/Edification into Satire or Rendered Exemplified

Unimportance…………………………Importance
Unwarranted Opinions……………Qualified Stance
Before Freedom………………………After Freedom
Before Liberty…………………………After Liberty
Criminal Intent…………………………Civil Liberty

Criminal Abuse…………………………Civil Discussion

*Experience or Sensibility: media category and maturity rating

Artistic Safeguards

If you want controversial media approved, revise satirical consideration, maintain integrity guidance

*Guidance set in differing eras, or otherwise tested within the extreme, may require fiction status/genre

Intellectual ability of audiences has been safeguarded or tested, or technically downgraded

* Media category and maturity rating

Careful authoritative designs, blatant misuse of concept, imitation of authoritative dystopia
* Media category and maturity rating

Social programs to enable content formation

* Media category and maturity rating

Civics Academia

As pro civics, advanced intellectual arts as liberal, and science with clear funding sources, both with premise:

Categorizes relevant to funding as

Cultural Relevancy (Liberal Arts as guidance, explanations)

- Archives proving civilization
- Political proving short term
- System displaying active model and normalcy (custom regional)
- Experimental exemplifying pivotal (propose pivotal as performance)
- Empirical intelligence such as automated intelligence, designing
- Civics configurations as organized social functions
- Steller

Scientific Relevancy

Structural Powers

- 1 Media
- 2 Education (Regulating Knowledge)

...

- 1 Justice
- 2 Military

...

- 1 Production
- 2 Government

...

- 1 Civics
- 2 Faith

It could be reasoned, that from refining observation, that we may observe the structural powers as having two levels of existence, in which they relate more directly, yet as vitals are integrated require each other as a thereby structure of power.

Notice 1 is the experimental and in that manner originator of 2

Notice 2 is the source as having priorities over 1, such as within developing from freedom to securements of liberty

Notice 2 are each long term, in relation to 1

Notice 2 are more difficult to alter altogether, require more paperwork, policy, adherences, than 1

*stable/experimental of 1 is from public feedback, causing 2 to be a naturally safeguarding organization, order of operations. (Relative to the scheduling, timed nature of content)

With feedback pivotal to all levels/layers of the proposed structure of powers, safeguarding the sensibility of public conformity, conditioning of sensitivity, reinforces each area of the structural powers is essential to the overall social validity constructed, and thereby abridging judgement, determination, onto stellar in cultural relevance/affirmation of destiny.

As ideal, civics is configured to enable experience, enable measure into determination which as emotionally driven, is enabled by priorities culturing/conditioning, such as in relation to **cultural relevance** and **scientific relevancy**. Thereof, faith is included, such as faith derived the formulation enabling civics as a judgement binding to validate determination, and determination requiring judgement as foundation, intellectual support structured.

Faith was used to originate formulation found in this text as civics considerations, as industry relevant conceptual, and thereby required bound within the formulation as both conclusion to judgement and determination, and in relation to validations of own foundation/founding-purpose.

Civics Determination of Faith

- Comprehension, objective as in determination of fundamental judgement values
    - As custom regional, adhering formal doctrines of established cultural and scientific relevancy (realistic, affirming leeway of connectivity)
- Adaptive as within framework meant across vast amounts of time
- Worship as means for citizenry to explore, intentions as safe kept in consideration of integrity as judgement formula
- Conservative as civics reinforcement of faith, such as within recycling,
- Commutability of faith, as in complex, layered and similarity towards biology and technology

Civics Determination of Conservative
(Default Civics as Pro Faith Defence)

Civics Determination of Conservative, ideally, as a demonstration that governance cares about resources. Default Civics as Pro Faith Defence as an abridgement between government and production is that of an abridgement of faith and civics, and further as promoted through media and education, defended by justice and militants, as an overall systemic, layered approach of self-determination, held/strengthened by a conceptual core as indoctrinated.

With Acari as a civics means to securement, thereby data storage as sacred, keeps backups and operational knowledge concerning vitals used for, across structural powers:

- Citizen ID
- Licensing Information/Registration
- Formalities of facilities
- Securements relating to physical materials, processing, storage standards
- Service descriptions and operational detail relating/promoting to increasing durability
- Arts, science and/as luxury details, such as in models developed/stored, custom regional arrangements relating to satisfying positions of authority

The technological pursuit of Acari systems, as the civics physical embodiment to this text, is that of enabling freedoms for operation in standard, relevant to technologies domestic in anticipation/direction to mobilization stellar: Yawaeh Systems.

Safeguarding of resource extraction itself, as well as methods and operational details, varies across many industries, such as onto tourism where the focus is directly upon experiences of an emotional arrangement, and either way, esteemed fashionable (assumed).

The predictably technological application, is to fabricate, maintain the environmental conditions in a manner where resources earned and resources used are calculated, yet the operational methodology are possibly highly valuable, such as for stellar performance. As (relatively) easy means to measure complex, and layered formations of operational undertaking.

*The default judgement-core reasoning, is that the projects remain within standards of health, with consideration as a system, that differing levels of potency render thus relative, the guidance thereof/therein provided.

Determination as civics focus on specialized pursuits/Interests

- Specialist industrial development as civics secured activities encouraging physical, intellectual labors
- Family cultivation of individual formations as encouraging physical, intellectual labors
- Tourism, service industries as providing/specialized in retrieve
- Custom reginal sensuality dedication as stability through organization, experimental
  - Contracting intellectual, physical secured judgment, as well as securing in terms of registration of facilitation of intellectual, physical secured determination

Determination as Civics Professions

- Resources reminder from civics that citizens do more than preform functions, they are cultivated and conditioning into layers of awareness, fulfillment, and encouraged into satisfaction
- Securing layers of industrial knowledge, livelihood across transformative upgrades to the infrastructure, especially within upgrading vitals
  - Upgrading the baseline defaults by providing options to work into, towards legacy (founding personas) figures
  - Being mindful other regions of the world require transitions of progress that require large scale development layers of reinforcing, supportive construction such as adapted to their regional resources as custom-rendering

Determination as State Configurations

- Creating short term political activation sequences where collective development plans attached to political motto being elected, enable democratic determination
- Reinforcement that survival of the technologically proficient requires a default amount of resources that as set within defaults of configuration, are elevated within the satisfactions of liberty, in which the political promise to prioritize emerging developmental cycles in conformity to an organized, coherent, compatible as reasonable.
- Voicing affirmations (requirements) in relation to reason and integrity (judgment) as to demand, vote into action determination towards extreme
- Status of leading within a multinational arrangement, reinforces technological vitals as at emergency level in relation to non-leading nations, whom may by contrast have lax views, considerations, and thereby can, should be approached with long term power-resource plans for the ameliorations enabling stellar conformities of a nevertheless centralized within civics arrangements.
  - Meaning trying to develop other regions into the leading nation's current conformity, is not possible (predictably), by the time the projects are built, the lead is already onto new generations of versions of adaptability, such as from diversified operations enhancing.
    - If the outwards development is not an enhancing feature, then such as through political, yet secured by state configuration, expansion is slowed or blacked until compatibility is restored/established

-

-

Civics Determination as State Configurations

Integration vs. Edification

- General requirements to older doctrines be adhered to, with integrity doctrines as lead filtering potential, such as by introducing ne layers of structural power to finally organized, process and operate all kinds of task and performance requirements their old paperwork cannot comply with
- Civics censorship defaults as art over graffiti, pro nationalism as structural powers allocated default gaming, media,
- Inner structural powers reserved usage, such as bound by formalities therein, exemplifying operational standards, offering collective insights, favoring appeals to civics determination
- Determination of civics as attempted beyond judgement, meaning judgement is adhered to, and projected destinations, destiny as long term and short term evaluated through enhanced performance

Civics Determination as Culture

- Technological pursuit as the esteem to what liberty is, as defining cultural perspective
    - Integrity bound as ecologically bound/sound
- Forging trade policy, as well as corporate and business incentives along projected and fulfilled traditions building to enhance domestic as capital technical lead interest
- Media driven as promoting essential to life, liberty resolutions
- Securities as positive affirmation of technological pursuit, a structural powers overall esteem towards a balance between/among encoding/encryption, and formalities, premise
- Securing context for the enabling of contractual formalities, such as enabling capital areas, exposition sites, networking displays as heritage areas, including centralizing areas into touristic and educational sites (or otherwise themed by structural powers and cultural relevancy) to a designated area, while working with, such as modify (as to adapt) existing surface areas to maintain or transfer commerce across/along considerations of capped market values
    - Change of fabrics and redevelopment into much larger areas, as meaning relative size and importance equates substantial move (potential state moving benefit for mass development as well as buy in features for local cultural assets/productions)
- Fixing celebrations to specific building locations, projects, including scale(occupancy size) of overall area (declaring movable festivities)

Civics Determination as Upgrading

- Upgrading as feedback relevant to wellbeing, as indicator of domestic peace
    - Equities leeway as developing what persona exemplifying trends
    - Requesting contextual information in reports, or noteworthy forwarded

Capital/Social   **Civics**

Domestic

Value/Demand   Establishes Reserves

Ownership Priced/Size   Survival Price Established

Luxury Price/Function   Industrial Priority Established

International-Empiric

Commodity/Demand   Exchange Reserves

Production/Capability   Development Potential

Luxury/Trade Leeway   Reserves Potential

Steller

Steller/Mobilization   Civics Ready

Fundamental Determination as Integrity Formulation

Conceptual Core (Premise Foundation)

Long-term Stability – Civics- Faith Reserves

Being Healthy determined as Integrity Ideals, a Systematic Approach, as meaning a framework of ideas centralized as functional in termination of overall fulfillment of categories, as it's conclusive upgrading, upkeep as the wholesome feature: The ideal framework of health as systematic awareness, as conceptual, systems basis to judgement-core.

Doing Health as (Contextually Driven)

Short Term Adaptive – Politically Driven/Applicable

Doing Healthy Determination as

- Promoting Individual and social boundaries

- Enhancing field beauty, actively within state configuration

- Esteems on fulfillment of relationship standards

- Cultivating through infrastructure as civics matter

- Faithful as samples, example, and models used within securement of healthy determination

- Safekeeping production vitals in functioning of enhancement features cultured

- Maintaining wholesome as upgrading as arising, mindful of stellar as destiny in design, conformity compute, conclude/abridge

*Individuals as in formation to lifestyles, and their relevance and in conforming to each other (civics usage, the admiration of examples as confirming to layered supports approach

* Segmented as options, elections relevant

Civics Integrity

Conclusive, Collective-Configuration/Embodiment

As universally applied/applicable, Integrity has several formation/formula. As universal, its (Integrity) ability to exist and be relevant across all judgement subject matter as a stable reference guiding measure/operations-design, then an overall configuration of, for being and doing necessitates this doctrine as covering the resources section, indicating a fortification of will version called divinities core..

Examining Integrity Formula as applicable in layers (social: judgement core, Civics: determination core, Divinity: Command, mobilization).

Healthy

Socially: That Health as fundamental extends into the significant of all ideals

Civics-Civil: That health as a leading component of judgement, applies onto all civics matters as measurable

Divine: That health has been identified as of core important to the meaning of all things/life

Beautiful

Socially: Centered on terms of health, the individuality of health reflects variance projected

Civics-Civil: That beauty relates to judgement, and is nevertheless function based literal

Divine: That the importance of beauty endures, onto, as everlasting

Loving

Socially: Interweaves judgement aspects of resource, references and determination of will core to expansion

Civics-Civil: In determination of long term self and collective cultivation plans

Divine: Enhancing depictions promoting the mobilization of virtue

Dignified

Socially: In determination of long term self and collective cultivation plans

Civics-Civil: Functions orientated as in relation to larger production formations

Divine: Enabling of automated intelligence within the formation of civics and infrastructure itself

Productive

Socially: The enabler of overall civilization as grouping of completed systems united/uniting

Civics-Civil: The facilitation of both stability and enhancing experiential

Divine: The emergence of core towards the restoration, establishing of God's direction

Faithful

Social: Long term bounds, in edification of transitional

Civics-Civil: Long term bound, displayed as short term abridgement to custom regional

Divine: An overall model, sample establishing direction

Truthful

Socially: Point of intellectual, policy maturation, status of references

Civics-Civil: Point of physical in addition to default intellectual, policy maturation, status of references

Divine: Command and mobilization as cultural, mechanically applied (universal defaults)

Wholesome

Socially: Wellbeing and in respects to upgrading

Civics-Civil: Wellbeing embedded into the default of structuring and its intelligence/perspective

Divine: A collectors of completed fulfillments, of compartmentalized adaptive

Socially: That Health as fundamental extends into the significant of all ideals

Civics-Civil: That health as a leading component of judgement, applies onto all civics matters as measurable, involved as survival reserves and collective across systems offering prosperity defaults

Divine: That health has been identified as of core important to the meaning of all things/life

...

Civics Healthy as a conclusive formula for Judgement Core (Rising as collective in comprehension approved)

As healthy relates to enabling the body to function

Civics Defaults:

Public health as most reasoning to safeguard the largest amount of bodies, displayed as per likely positive-influence for targeted age/maturity groups

- Especially obvious to segments where reduction lowers grievances
- Promoting the style as common themed actions found generally beneficial
- Contextual as focusing on participation of interest
    o Cultivation: Promoting known calibrations to be fruitful/productive
    o Nurture default: Fuels of Resources, also in relation to maintain
    o Defensive allocation: assuring longevity
    o Injured status as necessarily assumed not knowing what is needed, as to be tended to not guided
    o Injury as disruption meaning there is a need to reform as to not compromise
- The observation of context, also in relation to holdings secured, to regional academia, and structural powers recommendations/allowances
    o In network of sampler, observation tools
    o Devices to enable system to respond, dedicated maintainers of sensory additions, enhancers (possible Archives relevancy)
- Exploring taste, enjoyment of tastes as sanctioned, feedback setups
    o General food and environmental monitoring through regional sampling based on large volumes of usage
    o As good taste, a sense of being alive in the supportive across various levels of operations offering fulfillment
        ▪ Imagery in relation to attributing, as raising esteems of themes building reference
        ▪ Poetic adherence, formalities of intellectual or contextual symbolism
            • Potential need to justify interpretation in relation to records

Civics Defaults – Memory Storage

Healthy as Memory

Memory with added self-status is embedded, an experience with emotion as result to signal, such as from detachment (similar to adding light display when operational)

- Topic of display memory signaled upon unplug
- Symbols priority remembering, brands/registered class as included potentially in added
- Per structured power as governance-fields/property districts, usage
- Network capability as to endure/execute as send only, secured recovery (library default)
- Layers of access each with backup into achieving next area, if common room placed
    - Frequencies
    - Power, reserves status

Healthy as Memory

Formulated into Esteems

Civics locked into services

Political mass usage of resource, heritage engineering

Databases:

- Complete status as Knowledgeable
- Display status as operational

In Field Support:

- Model examples/forms
- Policy, reference access
- Civics & Faith Defaults
    - Differing categories of traditions (access, privilege) forging
    - United in the relevance
    - Wholesome as contained, and thereof upgrade

*In consideration of Data, such as from Integrity Matrix

Integrity Matrix Data Template
Truth as Data Central

Healthy (Functional body) -

*Truth as bodily configurations, such as to bypass, technological as ecology benefits

Beauty (Functional deciphering of sensual stimuli)

*Truth as organs reactions specific, sensibility repeating model cycles

Loving (Functional emotion reaction in relation to situation / circumstance, safeguarding expression / actions)

*Truth as layered in particular of previous, concludes and strategic formations

Dignified (Functional relationships, safeguarding interaction)

*Truth as signed up for, as specifically agreed upon, formation of relationship premise

Civilization (Providing a supportive infrastructure, direction, maintenance, safeguarding individuals /society)

*Truth as citizen, with opportunities to excel/advance or rise as acceleration, of membership, in relation to access, esteem and privileges

Faith (Affirmation of understanding / enhancement of sensual- emotional self-actualization)

*Truth as guidance, with a forward, accuracy able to exemplify predictions

Productive – Functional lifestyles, from profession to procreation (Safeguarding long-term traditions of talent, and biological continuation)

* Truth as mentionable, strategic evaluations talent

Wholesome as Upgrading be default of maintaining, adjusting, formations

*Truth as applicable, mentioned as guidance poetic, or otherwise conclusive on common clarifications (predictably advised)

Truth as then explaining, to fill in the following:

Archives - Explanations of physical components to health

System - Body as Having Physical Intelligence and Intellectual: **configurations**

Supreme - Layered Healthy (**formulas** based from system observations/awareness)

Stellar – As the potency of **faith, biology, technology** enable

Consider the infrastructure remains, enact as functional/functioning

- Service detail - To remain stocked and prepared, or pending (secured as potency adjustable)
- Service functioning, powered, maintained
- Constituted for the environment conditioned into/for/motivational

Adjustment of service detail and center of functioning, as themed, contracted

Infrastructural Vitals

- Festive areas as huge stimulants for the look, arrangement, preparations across the landscape
  - Per structural power as infrastructural dominance

Civics Ideals - Beautiful as Retrieve
Rejuvenate Through Services

- Resting options to replenish strength
- Coordination to reinforcing events
- Raising quality of sleep (noise reduction)
- Pro diets, purposeful meal combinations
- Soothing aches, influencing moods
- Deprive/reform focus potential as restore premise purpose, maintain core considerations
  - Highlight or untangle clutter, refocus as better angle of entry/identification
- Recreation and personal time as having options organized from civics, maintaining individual quality, maintaining regional conformities, maintaining as civics feature
- Reflecting on the brain as fragments and as whole, from inner experiences, to ideas generated within layers therein experienced further,
- Dreams, and dreams interpretation, inspirational
  - Movement theorems, sensory experiences
- Self-refinement Intellectual, emotional, component/technologies driven
- Conditioning projects
- General leeway towards creation,
- Culture centre promoting societal aspects (active, current parts of heritage)

*Removing dystopia projections displayed, exemplified, protecting general public interest

Civics Ideals - Loving as Careful
Well Being Through Cheerful

- Responses as in the positive, as in reinforcement of formalities of loving commitments, and their particular arrangements,
- Response leeway enabled from the formalities received, presented, and the approach positive to those statements as freedoms of speech, freedom of being, and freedom of privacy,, in a complex and layered consideration
- Careful selection in relation to solutions building, solutions providing as themselves in relation to public allowances, such as versus privet conversations

Healthy Prioritization (Functional bodies relating)

*Priorities as bodily configurations, such as to bypass, technological as ecology benefits

Beauty (Functional deciphering of sensual stimuli)

* Priority as organs reactions specific, sensibility repeating model cycles

Loving (Functional emotion reaction in relation to situation / circumstance, safeguarding expression / actions)

* Priority as layered in particular of previous, concludes and strategic formations

Dignified (Functional relationships, safeguarding interaction)

* Stimulation/dedication as signed up for, as specifically agreed upon, formation of relationship premise

Civilization (Providing a supportive infrastructure, direction, maintenance, safeguarding individuals /society)

* Priority as citizen, with opportunities to excel/advance or rise as acceleration, of membership, in relation to access, esteem and privileges

Faith (Affirmation of understanding / enhancement of sensual- emotional self-actualization)

* Priority as guidance, with a forward, accuracy able to exemplify predictions

Productive – Functional lifestyles, from profession to procreation (Safeguarding long-term traditions of talent, and biological continuation)

* Priority as mentionable, strategic evaluations talent

Wholesome as Upgrading be default of maintaining, adjusting, formations

* Priority as applicable, mentioned as guidance poetic, or otherwise conclusive on common clarifications (predictably advised)

Civics Ideals - Loving as Careful
Loving Through Rejuvenation

- Learning regulation into experiences, as having to strengthen vigor, as character formation in relevancy of conditioning (typical standard)
- A default of logics, judgement as perhaps vague compared to determination, yet clear in the direction overall of premise vs. of focus derived assumed soundly
- Culturing loving as relating to priorities, and of respecting the prioritization between people to forge dignified relationships
- Social, cultural recollection as experiences bound, shared, active culture as remembered vital heritage points
- Determination as deciphered, whereas judgement guides values, determination as structured, already involving systems implemented, operations of valued united
    - Loving assumes completed, formal systems assigned memberships are valid
- The needs of determination already involving matured states of input, contribution, civics as already established resources, references, and as testament in virtue of will sanctified (long term adhered)
- Whereas judgement-core is about precedence building precedence, Acari as determination core is about bound, social into civics cultured networks implemented into operating,
    - A functional model in design as nevertheless sound in judgement
- The promotion of production as physical manifestation of judgement, celebrated as civics as bound to reserves, as relevant to secured factors themselves considered into involvement/cheer
- Encouraging the deciphering of systems in explainable, established recognition having sensibilities added as devices are guided sound in template.
    - Whereas template enable variance made compatible, having options as relevant to custom regional resources, references, and will as terms or ease of usage in relation to structured powers (predictably)
- Freedom of speech within civics, as membership privilege, access within formalities mentioned, stated as chosen regulation, as means to control and therein assumed to refine
- Intellectual concerns as educational or be default assigned by stature powers
- Emotional conditioning as regional custom, yet media exemplified as emergency examples/considerations required (establishing reason, through media applied)
- Determination as buildings solutions, purpose of specific buildings initiated as collaborations, enablers

Civics Ideals - Loving as Careful
Survival-Defaults - Reactive

- Public calm despite anger: Determination to rid of a disruption, leeway in accordance to negative guidance, or in disregard from arrangement/behaviour, context is public policy guiding is not being adhered
- Stupidity found, as multiple testing of same or general conditions, of which the testing itself is not permitted, been provide and accepted as wrong on terms of previous warnings
- Increase in public measure in determination the actions found are part of patterns of action which conflict against an individual and social policy.
    - Discard that the mobilization to monitor or intervene isn't itself an infraction. Yet as relevant to formalities, possibly resourced and referenced as multinational intrusive
- Total removal as in determination of infrastructural defences, obvious mobilization, permissions
- Memorial sites as in relevance to strategic considerations of networked infrastructural defence
- Media depiction of large scale refugee, and other mass relocations relevant
- Heritage as needful considerations, active operations acknowledgement
- Heritage as in esteem to principals, criteria orientated
- Displays of public character, forms to use

Civics Ideals - Loving as Careful
Quality of Life – Reactive

- Resolutions reactions as in measure of functional and durability
    - Functional as not requesting, undertaking as responsive
    - Durable as not in distress

*Resolving as a defensive and nurturing conclusions rendering

*Spiritual as in influence of others as collective grace, of mindful, collective

System determination as pledges, assumes nevertheless an accuracy in formalities

Civics Ideals – Dignified as Fulfilling

Quality of Life – Reactive

Dignified as integrity layered into conditions accepted, developing of fulfillment, and satisfaction values for life. As structural powers, or cultural and scientifically relevant, the fulfillment is relevant to differing placed, placement values assumed for, towards attaining refinement for specialized interest rendering (resources, references, determination of will (specific/specialist)

Healthy Stimulation/dedication (Functional bodies relating) -

*Stimulation/dedication as bodily configurations, such as to bypass, technological as ecology benefits

Beauty (Functional deciphering of sensual stimuli)

* Stimulation/dedication as organs reactions specific, sensibility repeating model cycles

Loving (Functional emotion reaction in relation to situation / circumstance, safeguarding expression / actions)

* Stimulation/dedication as layered in particular of previous, concludes and strategic formations

Dignified (Functional relationships, safeguarding interaction)

* Stimulation/dedication as signed up for, as specifically agreed upon, formation of relationship premise

Civilization (Providing a supportive infrastructure, direction, maintenance, safeguarding individuals /society)

* Stimulation/dedication as citizen, with opportunities to excel/advance or rise as acceleration, of membership, in relation to access, esteem and privileges

Faith (Affirmation of understanding / enhancement of sensual- emotional self-actualization)

* Stimulation/dedication as guidance, with a forward, accuracy able to exemplify predictions

Productive – Functional lifestyles, from profession to procreation (Safeguarding long-term traditions of talent, and biological continuation)

* Stimulation/dedication as mentionable, strategic evaluations talent

Wholesome as Upgrading be default of maintaining, adjusting, formations

* Stimulation/dedication as applicable, mentioned as guidance poetic, or otherwise conclusive on common clarifications (predictably advised)

<u>Stimulation/dedication as then explained to fill in the following:</u>

Archives - Explanations of physical components to health

System - Body as Having Physical Intelligence and Intellectual: **configurations**

Supreme - Layered Healthy (**formulas** based from system observations/awareness)

Stellar – As the potency of **faith, biology, technology** enable

Civilized

Civilized as configuration in facilitation, regional infrastructure potential, what does your membership in one area or another imply

Civilization (Providing a supportive infrastructure, direction, maintenance, safeguarding individuals /society)

Healthy Civilized: Artistry **(Functional pro infrastructural as body)**
* **Artistry** as bodily configurations, such as to bypass, technological as ecology benefits

Beauty (Functional deciphering of sensual stimuli)

* **Artistry** as performance specific, sensibility repeating titles profiled

Loving (Functional emotion reaction in relation to situation / circumstance, safeguarding expression / actions)

*Truth as layered in particular of previous, concludes and strategic formations

Dignified (Functional relationships, safeguarding interaction)

* **Artistry** as signed up for, as specifically agreed upon, formation of relationship premise

Civilization (Providing a supportive infrastructure, direction, maintenance, safeguarding individuals /society)

Artistry as citizen, with opportunities to excel/advance or rise as acceleration, of membership, in relation to access, esteem and privileges

Faith (Affirmation of understanding / enhancement of sensual- emotional self-actualization)

* **Artistry** as guidance, with a forward, accuracy able to exemplify predictions

Productive – Functional lifestyles, from profession to procreation (Safeguarding long-term traditions of talent, and biological continuation)

* **Artistry** as mentionable, strategic evaluations talent

Wholesome as Upgrading be default of maintaining, adjusting, formations

* **Artistry** as applicable, mentioned as guidance poetic, or otherwise conclusive on common clarifications (predictably advised)

Artistry as then explaining, to fill in the following:

Archives - Explanations of physical components to health

System - Body as Having Physical Intelligence and Intellectual: **configurations**

Supreme - Layered Healthy (**formulas** based from system observations/awareness)

Stellar – As the potency of **faith, biology, technology** enable

Faithful as symbolic embodiment, of universal appeal, or regional reinforcement as a collective whim

Truthful as Passion

Destiny as Objectivity
Truth as a Civics ideal, has layers of recognition.

Archives

- Truth as guidance
- Truth as direction, such as experimental guidance

System

- Truth as System directions
- Truth as trends, and emerging innovative

Administrative within system

- Truth as intelligence configuration
- Truth as civics compatibility and user connectivity

Research and Development (long term trajectory therein)

- Truth as destiny, stellar

...

The truth as having multiple layers of function or priority within judgement-core, as enabling compartmentalization into specialist reinforced as design to system stability, and adaptor with advancing experimental

In relation to guidance, differing subject matters and means to approaching, introducing, using the knowledge, means help is complex, such as to convert and condition long term or to answer questions such conversation or conditioning enables as every day specialist ability/talent/profession?

Era as contextually driven knowledge, as requiring the answering system to hold all the answers as key or insight, yet to what invested interest is there in examination, or approval. What is the mutual trajectory forward?

Truth as mentioned in this text, if universal attributes to ideals, thus useful in focusing determination:

Quality

Artistry

Productive as integrity in relation to cultivating professional whim and passion with recreational reinforce, long term resource chosen support to enhance upgrade into

Wholesome as upgrading, in connectivity to refining pursuits, of templates, on premise designs both of being whole in relation to, and of knowing the enhancement features of compartmentalized adaptive

Properties found as stable/part of Ideals as archives, and so the results as integrating into system awareness:

(Overall Conceptually-Fulfilling (Indicator) Attributes Found within/with Ideals)

Durability……………………………………… (Health)

Satisfaction………………………………………..(Beautiful)

Artistry (Science defaults) ……………….(Civilization)

Stimulation/dedication ……………………..(Dignified-Relationships)

*Procreation as Universal Adaptive Pending

Esteem/Configurations………………………..(Production)

Priority/bound……………………………………. (Loving)

Whole/enhancing…………………………….…..(Faithful)

Upgrade/settings…………………….………..…..(Wholesome)

Judaic Soul		
Reincarnation	Incarnation	Reformation
Reason	Refinement	Strategy
Reference	Resource	Will
Social	Civics	Divinities

Civics Conditioning Amenities / Venue Selection

- Mental Preparation

  o Symbols exemplifying understanding
  o Conceptual diagrams (as book, program fragments)

Civics System Components

Pleasantries Sample

In the beginning there was desire for things, and they themselves began

Time as forming thicker, or being consumed such as with heat and (and from being in relation to another) force

The kindness felt at home, generally in arrangement to that regions formality using faith and that or those individuals entertaining/entertained

Rising voices of upgrade, the receipt onto inventory selections, of gifts in recollection

Rendering sacred names honored, in poetic across Medias of expression

- Ceremonies were the material fabric I he ash absorbed into the skin is pleasant, welcome, useful
In the broadcast of echo, as in network, of communications (as an instillation, as a sanctuary, indicator)

- Sorting about deciphering, the distinguishing of/between, as the comparative using a measure. Establishing measures as the context of the premise, or in the principal detail, were limitations old
- Mapping as into display, schedules, as to personify sound (themed music accord, networked as per selection (: co dependant ID and affirmation conclusion)

Reservations as Sanctuary for Members/Animals (dedicated sites)

Criteria for admission/entrance/membership

- Based on overall age reached
- Areas dedicated to flying animals
- Areas dedicated to ground animals
- Areas with sea animals
- A place for odd yet cute, cute as adorable or endearing
- Fountains
- Swimming areas
- On site harvest, supplies cultivation
- Strategic reasoning for placement:
- Near council of regional power, to show compassion
- As strategic do not pass, or guarded barrier
- Seasonal Reserves, supplies (based on mass storage ease)

Supreme Structural Powers

Media-Civics Supreme default Examples (Focal points, production campaigns)

Justice: Live Duty

Military: Militia games

Media: Media Trivia

Education: Quiz Challenge

Government: Spotlight news

Faith: Biology, technology, faith

Civics: Configurations

Production: Products (and in relation to access from structural powers)

*Worthy as contextual to relevant power structure, training, traditions

*Having specific introductions made, such as in esteem to locations of heritage for the structure of power

*Access to stored inventory based on membership to supreme structure of power category/division

*Default gift or emergency allowance, such as transportation or refuge; with equipment or supply

*Emergency credit, emergency on site field work (potential priority on upper qualification)

*Emergency trade of comport or luxury, such as preapproved, as enabled in advance (options)

*Emergency trophies trade, selling, exchange (personal, formal collections)

Civic Default Public-Celebration Allocation - Ritual Traditions

- Wind as representing souls
- The star formation in relevance to the solar system and the galaxy as central focal point, of from the point of most illuminating in the sky appearing as background
- Power ritually symbolized by radiating light
- Victory celebration as feasting and drinking
- Tournament related marriage proposals. Announcements
- Celebrating house wives, victory moments (toasting, complimenting)
- Pilgrim's staff, walking cane, or other symbol to wear and have default, visitor approved status
- Crumpling of leaves, the spray of confetti, effects to announce end, completion, event focal point with time to otherwise depart
    - Package content

Burial Sites

- Visiting grounds
- Registration and visitation (Administrative network)
    - ID membership
    - 24 hour access potential
    - Tombs
    - Featured appearances (travel packages)
    - Eloquent paths
    - Minerals area, beauty pieces sold, sales allocation
    - Devices to monitor for mischief, cleverly installed, such as lodged in thick material

National Compatibility

- Use of ancient formality into agreed upon template adherence in all regions, whose formality enables the desire to preserve such as tradition, adding a culture of reinforced conditioning journeys
- God's favor, as in esteem to what premise, such as authored, such as of judgment core being a fulfillment in relation, in being ready validating the all mighty
- Development plans, in regards to multinational, binding accords (Empiric presence)
- Military celebrations in Spring
- An overall esteem to guide visitors well
- Sympathy towards national character, as in relevancy towards formal criteria and membership access
- A valid/default association of nationalism and flying

Hospital

- Equipment Specialties
- Supplies strategically enabled (area of fabrication, local materials supply)
- Nurse Core as knowledge Database (Archives)
- Doctors (travel benefit towards secured room, facilities)
- Network buy in plans, for travel and hospital needs combined
- Recovery Sites (duration vs. location requirements)
- Ventilation requirements
- Ventilation requirements specifically for transportation area
- Different body sized rooms, if applicable
    - Tools, equipment implications?

*Media must ask casual stories only (onsite)

Civic Landmark

Maintained vantage points, kindness in features

- For seeing far into the horizon
- Entry restrictions (weapons, armor)
- Experimental show/events site (assumed seasonal)
    - o Speaker setup
- Picnicking, lounging structure
- Devices against air attacks
- Chorus Structure (acoustic site)
- Holiday themes (rotating as storage, decorations)
- Honoring of hero
- Favor/chivalry: experimental
- Poetic Site (with guided explanation)
- The (ideal) beauty of woman/women
- Offerings (nature, fertility), ecological goodness
- Defense from wildlife if observation point
- Parks dedicated to operational whereabouts for structural powers
- Placed in boundary to forge objective feedback
- Monitored site for pick up, send off (semi touristic, such as informational)
- License to play live music at landmark site (easements)
- Approved wisdoms, for quick landmark creation
- Caution sign for uneven ground, or for transportation
- Indications for transportation
- Maiden landmarks as, willing to premise, or exploring romantic dedication plans
- Artistic leeway as foolish or frantic, yet in depth explanation, such as in relevancy to slogan/motto and premise (vaguer than historic, potential part of a continuity to heritage)
- Hot watered sanitation as networked, developed
- Communications interactive (possibly/regional integrated into other networks of connectivity)
- Spectacle/Events area (designation)
- On site solar, wind or water current powered energy (or other renewable, resource)
- Network connectivity

Connection to emergencies broadcast system
Tracking of foreign ID, Touristic Highlights, packages resources reminders updates
Feedback

Civic Landmark – Historic

- Depicting earlier formation, details
- Explaining the development, progress
- Explaining relevant experimentation/discovery

Civic Landmark

- Signs for local resources, services
  - o Fuel
  - o Eating
  - o Supplies//Equipment
  - o Hospital
  - o Civics program
  - o Information
  - o Local Services
  - o Local Industries
  - o Route Indications
  - o Recovery area

Detection of status of neglect

- Wear and tear along routes
- Frequency-infrequency highlight/alert
- Detection/connection with sanctuary network, civics network
- Issue with limbs, pieces, parts (moving)
  - o Noise indicator

Shelters – Base/Mobile Emergency Solutions

- For people in shock
- For people injured
- For waiting injured for a duration (recovery timing)
- Grieving sites
- Mechanisms to lock and release packages
  - o Easement to reload, refresh stock

Emergency Communication Database/Network

Consent request – license easement

Accuser – assistance call

Explanations to emergency situations

Emergency Packages

- Announcements
- Vestments

Journey Packages

- Regional selections
- Themed production sampling
- Themed civics arrangement/activity
- Romance reserves, dedicated journeys
- Honeymoon

General Packages

Containment options and transportation thereof arranged

- Lost and found system of recovery
- Tools collection
- Historical information, journey, routes
  - Intended popular

Tourism - Supreme Structures

- Old Military Instillations, palaces

- Dates

- Cataloging outer styles of material, patterns (modern recreations, theme buildings)

- Weathering process involved such a heat baked?

- Layers to foundations in original (can materials be changed to augment)

- Material mixes, new mixtures versus ancient, changes in durability

- Cataloging surface textures

- Smooth

- Shiny

Tourism - Symbolic Regional Custom

Fabrics and material quality standards

- Wearable symbols (material usable on flesh, prolonged usage tested)

- Chains durable (no fashion only chain, safety bounds)

- Decorative light weight supplies for regional custom artistic fabrications

- Beads

- Local stones as small, portable objects

- Heavier stone or heavy materials for static emplacement

- Vassals

- Largescale landscaping arrangements as indoors (protecting from erosion)

- Use of mouldable supplies fabric for outdoor usage

- Non degrading metals for kitchen, eatery

- Nontoxic clays, materials for pottery

- Basic impact durability as hard, flexibility durability as soft fabric usable

    - Dishes

    - Reusable, daily vitals

    *Significant recycling, composting (sustainable) programs as enabling leeway

Tourism - Museums places

- As justifying production
- Offering volumes of insights, considerations

- Highlighting generosity of owners, regional powers, managers of note (noteworthy as exemplified)

- Academic explanations areas or overall themes if formality of title premise

- Domestic becomes international collections, potential formality of title premise

- Date, dimensions detailing if applicable

- First models, first mass scaled operations/fabrications

        - Differing materials used

- Limitations and expansion into new fabrics, materials used (assumed developmental explanations)

- Original purpose of location, building, equipment, supplies as developed/developing

- Custom arrangements to facilitate themselves sources of innovation, if applicable

        - Interesting requirements, technical requirements: audience expected, financing relevancy

- Original site plans, vs./and development look, feel, experiences

- General adaptations

- Relevant local discoveries

- Sample rooms, model representative areas

        - Depicting era

        - Depicting local origins in production relevancy (as proficient)

Tourism - Museums places - Authenticity ironies

- Erosive, corrosive materials no longer used do to danger, so re-usage for display as non acceptable, not authentic as promoting production ideal

        - Alterations and reasoning included as conceptually driven, nor eroding experiences required

- Dealing with thieves, invasion

Themes of Focus - Filtering Content

Dynamic story telling formulas

- Mindful of exaggerations

    - Categorical as media fantasy-fiction or media historic

    - Puzzle formations mapped out

        - Criteria for unlocking through specific paths/avenues of transitions

- Outcome modified within selections chosen as adaptive/interactive components

- Creating solving mechanism, scenarios and answer to assemble into passages connecting options/decisions

- Decoding patterns, creating patterns unmasking trickery as learning themes or styles of designs

- Adapting volumes of storyline into premise formulations, such as transitions into new eras of learning/adaptation

- Establishing enjoyable reference points, highlighting known intrigues among volume selections/options rendering

- Compliance to formalities, such as touristic implementation

- Highlighting errors in instructions and results, casualties (through story telling)

- Exploring easily, or complex misleading

- Adventures of hope as attainable

- Exploring racial conditioning, highlights in differences: as highlighting specialized features

    - Potential re-examination of historical, past development to re-examine future developments predictable

- Exploring appearance stated versus experience driven

- Practical conditioning journeys

    - Academic

    - Discipline forging

    - Physical training

    - Talents and hobbies into membership and partition

- Exploring scope differences such as administrative along worker performance insights

    - Potential settings for viewer, user to participate with either, or both blended/contrasted

    - Language simplification/complexities

- Themed per structural power

- Detailing greatness or wonderment (fantasy enhanced)

- Explaining regulation as simplified and examples based

- Explaining historic territorial disputes

- Exploring eras of fashionable, establishing contextual

    - Contrasting

- Adapting to extreme conditionings, adapting to natural environments

- Cultivating the environment through technological purpose

- Fortune building

- Power management, models of might as influence rendering

    - Natural themes of magnitude as elite symbols reinforcing sceneries (assumed applicable)

- Exploring meanings as drought into illumination

- Faith dedications, long term dedication

    - Reinforcement through ritualized performance/depictions

- Reinforcing endurance principals/formulas for performance

- Examples of overcoming grief, establishing/re-establishing purpose

- Trance as poetic, artistic layering of senses, as sense of self overlapping story, abridging conclusions/depictions between being and doing

- Adaptive recovery

- Displaying quotes and passages into storyline lived through audience participation/contemplation

Note from Author

- This book honors my bloodline connection to Solomon, proving soul.

- This book requires the Judgement-Core Series to act as refinement tool

- This Book Fulfills the Acari systems as a Boundaries System mentioned in Judgement-Core

- This Book is made stand alone, and work in conjunction to Yawaeh Systems